Once Upon
a Child

TO OUR CHILDREN
Lawren, Meagan, and Mary Ryan
David, Finley, Cole, and Blair

"To be nobody but yourself—in a world which is doing its best, night and day, to make you everybody else—means to fight the hardest battle which any human being can fight; and never stop fighting."

e. e. cummings, "A Poet's Advice"

Many thanks to Judy Marine, principal of the Westminster Elementary School, for her help and encouragement in the very earliest stages of this book; and to my husband, George McChesney, for his patience in hearing the same "seven" pages read in many changing forms.

Published by
PEACHTREE PUBLISHERS, LTD.
494 Armour Circle NE
Atlanta, Georgia 30324

Text © 1995 by Debbie Donnelly McChesney
Illustrations © 1995 Sarah Gayle Carter

Excerpt from *THE LITTLE PRINCE* by Antoine de Saint-Exupery, copyright 1943 and renewed 1971 by Hardcourt Brace & Company, reprinted by permission of the publisher.

Excerpt from "Give a Little Whistle" featured in Walt Disney's *PINOCCHIO* © The Walt Disney Company.

"I'm Going to Say I'm Sorry," from *THE OTHER SIDE OF THE DOOR* by Jeff Moss. Copyright 1991 by Jeff Moss. Used by permission of Bantam Books, a division of Bantam Doubleday Dell Publishing Group, Inc.

Book and cover design by Nicola Simmonds Carter

10 9 8 7 6 5 4 3

Manufactured in Hong Kong

ISBN 1-56145-100-2

Once Upon a Child

Debbie Donnelly McChesney, M.Ed.

Illustrated by Sarah Gayle Carter

PEACHTREE

ATLANTA

*"B*ooks are the quietest and most constant of friends, they are the most accessible and wisest of counselors, and the most patient of teachers."

Charles Eliot, *The Happy Life*

How young we are when we begin to wonder who we are, what our friends and family think of us, and where we are heading. As a parent, it is difficult to love our children without unconsciously imposing our opinions and hopes on their dreams. In responding to them, we praise, criticize, and judge. *Once Upon a Child* is a path to finding the unique qualities in your child. It is a diary based on the belief that all children are good—honest, compassionate, full of wonder, and capable of living in harmony with each other and the earth.

"Ryan's Christmas pageant was tonight. While on stage, she was very nervous—white-faced and tight-lipped. Lawren winked at her, and Ryan relaxed and smiled....Magic."

Lawren,
December 21, 1993

What a wonderful gift to bestow on your child— a book of your thoughts, appreciation, and unconditional love. In its original form, this book is an open slate containing some thoughts from me, its author, some lovely illustrations from the artist, and lots of blank pages. It is my hope that each copy of this book becomes some child's special story.

*I*n twenty years of working with children and their families, first as a teacher and then as an educational therapist, I have observed an increasingly competitive world in which our children are tested, measured, and over-scheduled. Their time for unstructured, imaginative play is often limited to small segments squeezed into a hectic routine. In the pursuit of our children's academic excellence, athletic achievement, and exposure to the arts, we often unknowingly compromise the development of the whole child. As a society, we tend to emphasize and label these tangible aspects of our children's lives as all-important, while overlooking intangible qualities such as wonder, compassion, truth, and peace. I believe these four qualities, strong and intact, are essential for the building of character and self-esteem. They are the necessary cornerstones for future happiness.

Children see themselves through your eyes, your words, and your opinions. Through your personal attention and invested time, they develop an intrinsic sense of self-worth. Self-esteem gives each child the ability to say, "I am a good person." In accepting this fact about themselves, children set aside the need to impress others with negative behavior. They continue to trust in themselves and respond with spontaneity and joy to the world.

*T*he idea for *Once Upon a Child* is the result of a crossroads between my professional life and my role as a mother. As an educational therapist, I am continually reminded of the importance of self-esteem in children. As a mother of three, I realize the challenging task of recognizing and responding to each of my children's individual talents and gifts with enthusiasm, steering clear of empty praise. All three of my children have their own book which I have written in since they were small. I continue to find these journal books a place to pause and reflect on each child, alone. I often write on the compassionate spirit of Lawren, the playful imagination of Meagan, and the uncompromising honesty of Mary Ryan. Don't let me mislead you—my children don't even swing from the lowest branch of the perfect tree, but they have great moments, and those moments are many. There are times when the simplest of their gestures is so magnificent that all of their imperfections are invisible. These moments, evidence of their essential goodness, fill a book, just as drawings, clay pottery and various concoctions of aluminum foil, construction paper and glue fill a hope chest. Time buries treasures such as these unless you save them.

"I know why you lose teeth—so the fairies can come and get them and God can put them in the new babies' mouths."

Ryan, September, 1994

*Y*ou can capture your child's unique moments through writing anecdotes, stories, and quotes, but the uses of *Once Upon a Child* are limited only by your imagination. I sometimes write letters to my children in their books and leave them open on their bed, or encourage them to write a poem or story in their own books. Their books make wonderful bedtime reading, especially at the end of a difficult day. Please do not think of this book as a behavior modification tool or reward system. It is rather a mirror where children may see good reflections of themselves.

The stories you write in *Once Upon a Child* are not fairy tales fabricated in your imagination, but true accounts of your child's unfailing charm. What you write is a reflection of your child's special gifts: the time they rescued a hurt bird, played with a lonely child on the playground, or told the truth under stress. Keep in mind that children love to read and hear about themselves. Quotes, sentences, sentence fragments, or incomplete thoughts can become magical in the eyes of your child. As you record the good acts performed by your child, the story grows and your child recognizes him or herself as the hero or heroine of the book. Write often about efforts, not just successes. Show faith and trust in your child; write about his or her dreams.

After arriving in Jamaica, I said, "Look kids—they drive on the wrong side of the road!" I was quickly corrected by Lawren, who said, "No, Mom—not the wrong side of the road, just different."

Lawren, March 1993

*O*ne final note. My father was a man of few words. Perhaps it was because he was a man of many thoughts. Four years ago he died. What I have left of him are a few pictures and a few letters which I have stitched together to enhance my memories. In the years since my father's death I have come to realize the importance of his encouragement in times of difficulty. Mingled in with the grief is a wish for that feeling of support to have texture and realness. As the years stack up against these memories, his words become echoes distorted over time. *Once Upon a Child* will give permanence to your thoughts and truth to your child's memories. They will be able to relive those good moments, the feelings, the words and the color of the sky that day. And when you are finished writing they will have a part of you that will belong to them alone. Whether your child is four or forty, the words you write will sit patiently on the pages waiting to encourage, lift spirits, and fortify. It is often intimidating to write in a new, clean book, but take heart—this book truly begins only after your marks of lead and ink have been made. And when this book is old, torn and tattered, your simple words will be there through time and over distance, holding your love for each one of your children.

"I have to be honest because you trust me."

Meagan,
February, 1993

"But there is so little time to say things.
I am always putting away things that are too
real to say, and then they never get said."

Anne Morrow Lindbergh,
Hour of Gold, Hour of Lead

This Book Is All About

$\mathcal{A}$ sense of wonder is a child's portable playground. It is a way of seeing the world as an enchanted and exciting place. Through the eyes of a child, a scarf becomes a wedding veil or a fisherman's net. A split in the bushes can lead to a new dimension, an Indian footpath, or a palace courtyard. Children within their innocence are the master creators of dreams. They are glowing comets in a dark sky.

> Know you what it is to be a child? It is to be something very different from the man of today. It is to have a spirit yet streaming from the waters of baptism; it is to believe in love, to believe in loveliness, to believe in belief; it is to be so little that the elves can reach to whisper in your ear; it is to turn pumpkins into coaches, and mice to horses, lowness into loftiness, and nothing into everything, for each child has its fairy godmother in its own soul; it is to live in a nutshell and to count yourself king of infinite space.
>
> Francis Thompson, "Shelley Essay"

A child's desire to question, to learn, and to enjoy life stems from a spirit of curiosity and innocence. This fresh sense of awe leads to exploration and invention, where possibilities are endless. By writing the stories of your child's many wondrous encounters with the world, you make the profound statement that life soars with imagination and that innocence reveals truth. As parents, we confirm our children's wonder of the world. We give flight to their dreams.

"If a child is to keep alive his born sense of wonder without any such gift from the fairies, he needs the companionship of at least one adult who can share it, rediscovering with him the joy, excitement and mystery of the world we live in."
Rachel Carson, *The Sense of Wonder*

Compassion, at its most basic level, embraces the golden rule—"do unto others as you would have them do unto you." At its very best, it is the inner light that inspires us to end suffering and compels us to make sacrifices for others. It is the essence of heroism.

Compassion responds to the needs of others while enhancing the self-worth of the giver. Feeding a stray cat, drawing a picture for a bedridden grandmother, helping a lost child or showing concern for an injured team mate—each of these acts of kindness is a treasure. It is through these small deeds that children discover a generous heart can bring an enduring sense of contentment.

Through our opinions our children learn to appreciate the differences in others or to be threatened by them. They learn either the beauty of diversity or the narrow-mindedness of prejudice. Descartes wrote, "the chief cause of human errors is to be found in the prejudices picked up in childhood." As our world grows smaller and more closely knit, prejudice and its companion ideas become unnecessary burdens. When leaving childhood, two of the greatest gifts our children can take with them are open minds and loving souls.

"You never really understand a person until you consider things from his point of view—until you climb into his skin and walk around in it."

Harper Lee, *To Kill a Mockingbird*

Children approach the world with extraordinary candor. A child's honesty is clear-eyed, genuine, and at times astounding. It is spontaneous and free of inhibition. Children are militantly intolerant of shams and demand justice for the underdog. They fearlessly speak the truth on matters that would require immense courage from the bravest adult.

Imagine what a different world we would live in if somehow each child could hold on to that stubborn honesty and sense of justice into adulthood. Recording your child's acts of honesty, both small and courageous, shows that you value truth. When your children listen to you read about their truthful moments, they will feel confirmed as honest individuals. This affirmation will make dishonesty fit them like a pair of shoes two sizes too small.

As children grow, the situations that demand honesty will change, but a sincere commitment to truth can remain constant. To children with a strong conscience, honesty is the only reasonable option. They realize that to be dishonest is to betray a sincere heart. A child's honesty is a by-product of a parent's trust. Each entry you write is a clear message of trust in your child.

"Truth is tough. It will not break, like a bubble, at a touch; nay, you may kick it about all day like a football, and it will be round and full at evening."

Oliver Wendell Holmes, Sr., *The Professor at the Breakfast Table*

$\mathcal{A}$ peaceful spirit is born out of an inner strength, composed of self-awareness and self-confidence. It allows an individual to enjoy solitude as well as the company of friends. Even in a time of video games and cable television, children still gaze out the window, weave bracelets, and write poetry. Quiet time is their time to shut off the rest of the world, mold dreams for the future, and sort through the problems of the present. It is a time to restore the soul and fortify the spirit.

In solitude we discover the path to peaceful relationships, for it is only through self-knowledge that we begin to understand others. Comfortable with themselves, peacemakers display no need to assert power over others. They recognize that at times they must put aside their own wants for the harmony of the group. Whether giving up the front seat of the car to a sister or mediating an argument on the playground, the child who intervenes on behalf of peace is rare. Celebrate this precious gift in your child.

While learning to value peaceful relationships among their peers and family, children begin to understand the importance of humanity's quest for peace. Several of the Nobel Peace Prize Laureates have spoken with astonishing similarity on the link between peace among individuals and peace worldwide. In Elie Wiesel's 1986 Nobel speech, he voiced this common theme, saying, "Mankind must remember that Peace is not God's gift to his creatures, it is our gift to each other."

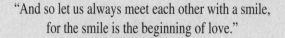

"And so let us always meet each other with a smile, for the smile is the beginning of love."

Mother Teresa, Nobel Peace Prize acceptance speech, 1979

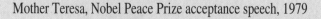

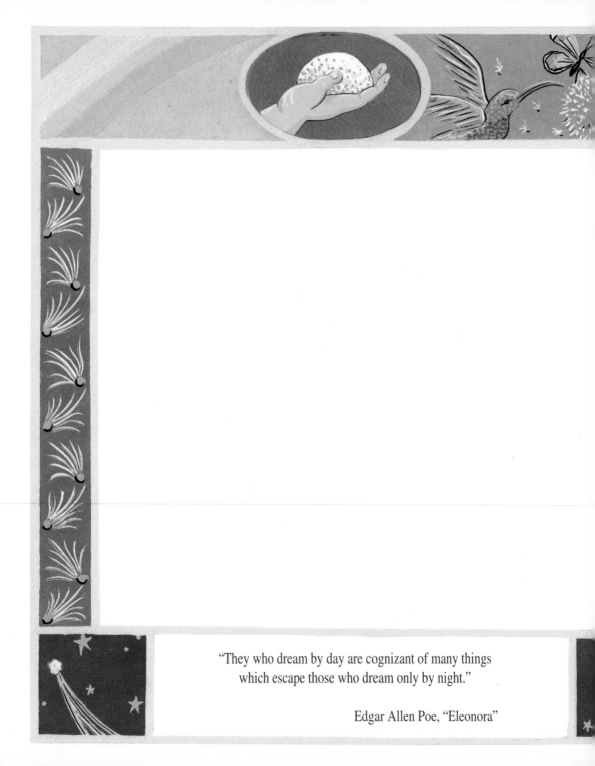

"They who dream by day are cognizant of many things
which escape those who dream only by night."

Edgar Allen Poe, "Eleonora"

"To know is nothing at all;
To imagine is everything."

Anatole France, *The Crime of Sylvester Bernard*

"'No, my head is quite empty,' answered the Woodman;
'but once I had brains, and a heart also; so, having tried
them both, I should much rather have a heart.'"

L. Frank Baum, *The Wizard of Oz*

"It is only with the heart that one can see rightly;
what is essential is invisible to the eye."

Antoine de Saint-Exupéry, *The Little Prince*

"To be what we are, and to become what we are capable
of becoming is the only end of life."

Robert Louis Stevenson,
Familiar Studies of Men and Books

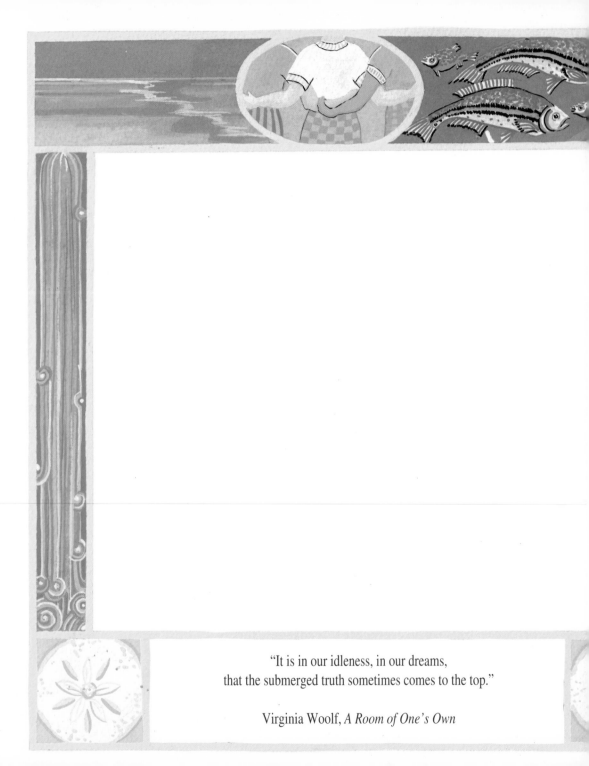

"It is in our idleness, in our dreams,
that the submerged truth sometimes comes to the top."

Virginia Woolf, *A Room of One's Own*

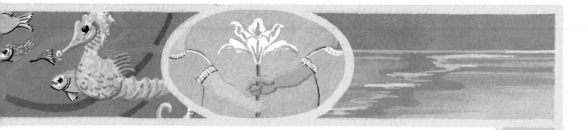

"I believe all religions pursue the same goals, that of cultivating human goodness and bringing happiness to all human beings."

The Dalai Lama, 1989 Nobel Peace Prize speech

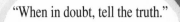

"When in doubt, tell the truth."

Mark Twain,
Pudd'nhead Wilson

"This above all: to thine own self be true, and it shall follow,
as the night the day—thou cans't not then be false to any man."

William Shakespeare, *Hamlet*

"No act of kindness, no matter how small, is ever wasted."

Aesop, "The Lion and the Mouse"

"It is my faith that compassion is the loveliest flower of the human spirit."

Archibald Rutledge, *Beauty in the Heart*

"The fairest thing we can experience is the mysterious. It is the fundamental emotion which stands at the cradle of true art and true science."

Albert Einstein, *The World As I See It*

"The most precious thing in life is its uncertainty."

Yoshida Kenko,
Essays in Idleness

"We love the things we love for what they are."

Robert Frost, "Hyla Brook"

"The supreme happiness of life is the conviction that we are loved."

Victor Hugo, *Les Misérables*

"…just about all children do have their strange, wondrous, luminous, brooding, magical, redemptive moments."

Robert Coles, *Privileged Ones*

"Every child is born blessed with a vivid imagination. But just as a muscle grows flabby with disuse, so the bright imagination of a child pales in later years if he ceases to exercise it."

Walt Disney, interviewed in
Wisdom: The Magazine of Lifetime Learning and Education

"May it be, oh Lord, that I seek not so much to be consoled as to console,
to be understood as to understand, to be loved as to love.
Because it is in giving oneself that one receives; it is in forgetting oneself
that one is found; it is in pardoning that one obtains pardon."

St. Francis of Assisi, "Admonition 27"

"My doctrine is this, that if we see cruelty or wrong that we have the power to stop, and do nothing, we make ourselves sharers in the guilt."

Anna Sewell, *Black Beauty*

"Give a little whistle...
and always let your conscience be your guide."

Jiminy Cricket, "Give a Little Whistle,"
song featured in Walt Disney's *Pinocchio*

"A good conscience is a continual Christmas."

Benjamin Franklin, *Poor Richard's Almanack*

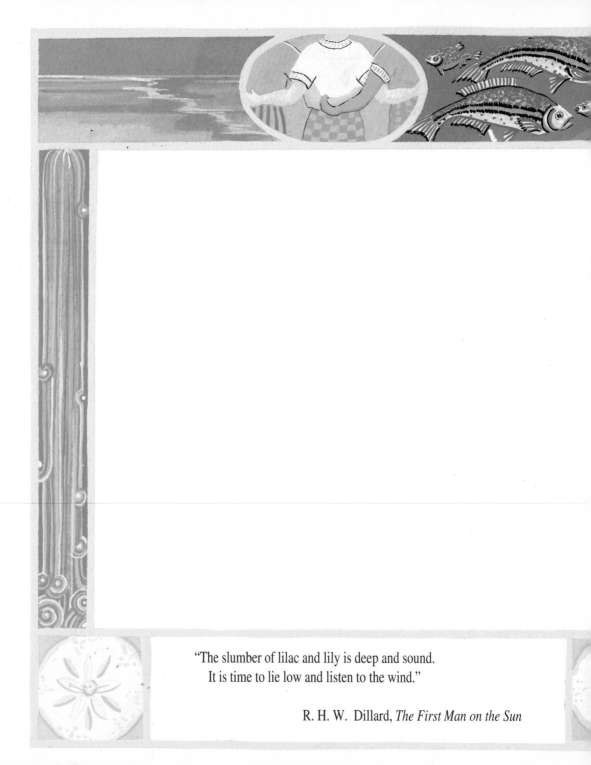

"The slumber of lilac and lily is deep and sound.
It is time to lie low and listen to the wind."

R. H. W. Dillard, *The First Man on the Sun*

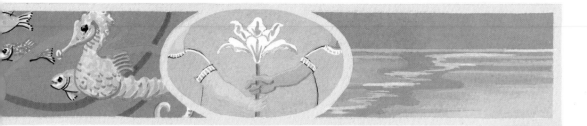

"…the great man is he who in the midst of the crowd keeps with perfect sweetness the independence of solitude."

Ralph Waldo Emerson, *Self-Reliance*

"Craft must have clothes,
but truth loves to go naked."

Thomas Fuller,
Gnomologia

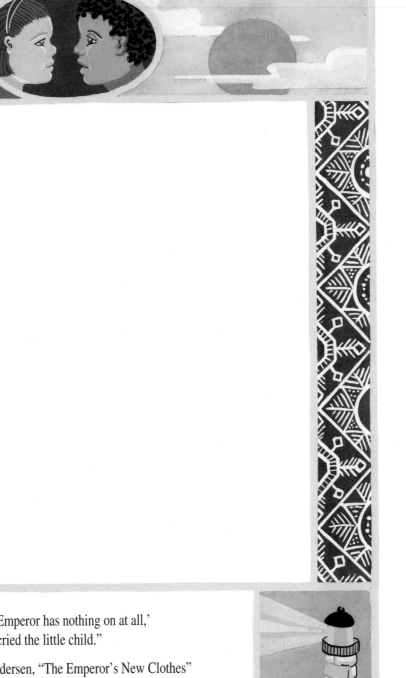

"'But the Emperor has nothing on at all,'
cried the little child."

Hans Christian Andersen, "The Emperor's New Clothes"

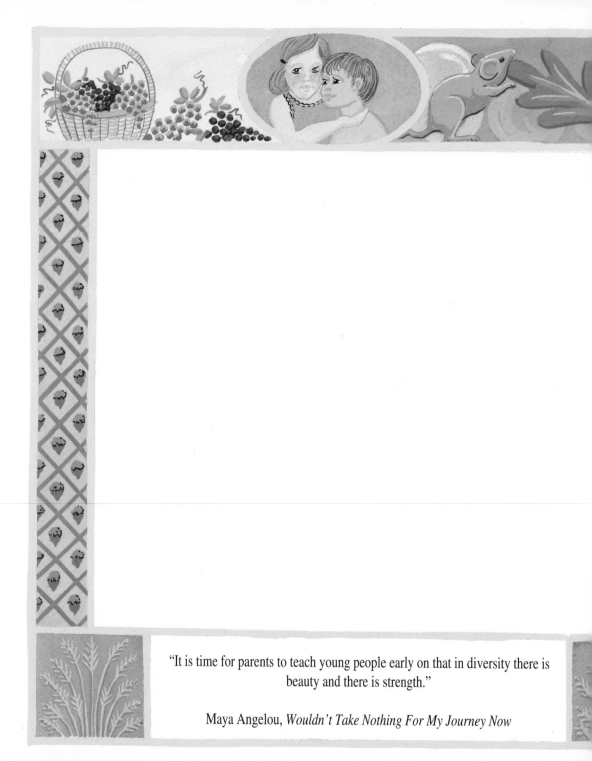

"It is time for parents to teach young people early on that in diversity there is beauty and there is strength."

Maya Angelou, *Wouldn't Take Nothing For My Journey Now*

"We shall be all alike—brothers of one father and one mother, with one sky above us and one country around us and one government for all. Then the Great Spirit will smile upon this land."

Chief Joseph of the Nez Perce,
in *Kopet: A Documentary Narrative of Chief Joseph's Last Years* by M. Gidley

"One doesn't discover new lands without consenting to lose sight of the shore for a very long time."

André Gide, *The Counterfeiters*

"I wonder whether all living isn't set to music, and whether the chief difference between happy people and unhappy people doesn't lie in their ears."

Channing Pollock, *Adventures of a Happy Man*

"We desperately need to remember that
we are each part of one another."

Madeleine L'Engle, *Two-Part Invention*

"If a man be gracious and courteous to strangers it shows he is a citizen
of the world, and that his heart is no island cut off from other lands,
but a continent that joins to them."

Francis Bacon, *Essays in Goodness and Goodness of Nature*

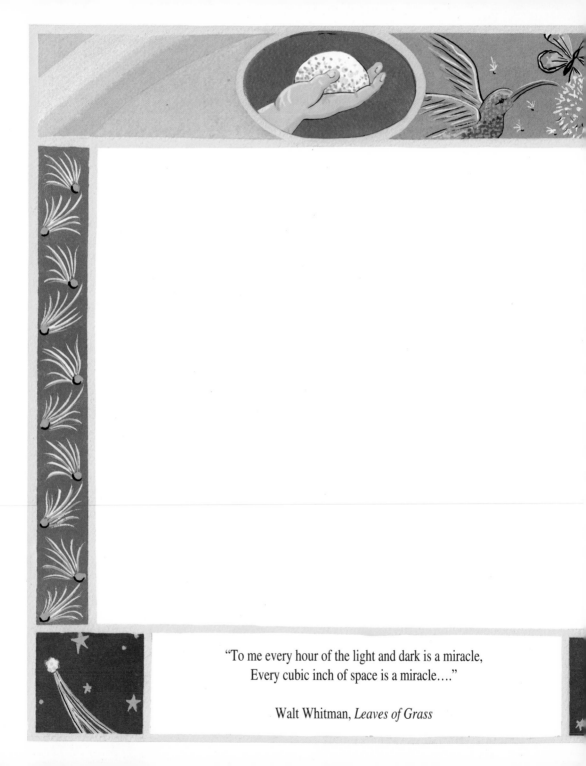

"To me every hour of the light and dark is a miracle,
Every cubic inch of space is a miracle…."

Walt Whitman, *Leaves of Grass*

"If I had influence with the good fairy who is supposed to preside over the christening of all children I should ask that her gift to each child in the world be a sense of wonder so indestructable that it would last throughout life."

Rachel Carson, *The Sense of Wonder*

"We can't form our children on our own concepts; we must take them and love them and love them as God gives them to us."

Johann Wolfgang von Goethe, *Hermann and Dorothea*

"Anything you do not give freely and abundantly becomes lost to you.
You open your safe and find ashes."

Annie Dillard, *The Writing Life*

"Truth never damages a cause that is just."

Mahatma Gandhi,
Non-Violence in Peace and War

"So absolutely good is truth,
truth never hurts the Teller."

Robert R. Browning,
"Fifine at the Fair"

"But there is neither East nor West, Border, nor Breed, nor Birth,
When two strong men stand face to face, tho' they come from
the ends of the earth!"

Rudyard Kipling,
"The Ballad of East and West"

"Occasionally in life there are those moments of inutterable fulfillment which cannot be completely explained by those symbols called words. Their meanings can only be articulated by the inaudible language of the heart."

Dr. Martin Luther King, Jr., 1964 Nobel Peace Prize speech

"Two things fill the mind with ever new and increasing wonder and awe—
the starry heavens above me and the moral law within me."

Immanuel Kant, *The Critique of Pure Reason*

"Truth may be stretched, but cannot be broken,
and always gets above falsehood, as oil does above water."

Miguel de Cervantes, *Don Quixote*

"The sad truth is that most evil is done by people
who never made up their minds to be either good or evil."

Hannah Arendt, *The New Yorker*, December 5, 1977

"Those who don't believe
in magic will never find it."

Roald Dahl,
The Minpins

"You never enjoy the world aright, till the sea itself floweth in your veins, till you are clothed with the heavens, and crowned with the stars; and perceive yourself to be the sole heir of the world."

Thomas Traherne, *Centuries of Meditations*

"For there is a fellowship more quiet even than solitude, and which,
rightly understood, is solitude made perfect."

Robert Louis Stevenson,
Travels with a Donkey in the Cevennes

"The soul is the sense of something higher than ourselves,
something that stirs in our thoughts, hopes and aspirations which go
out to the world of goodness, truth, and beauty."

Albert Schweitzer,
Reverence for Life; The Words of Albert Schweitzer

"The great instrument of
moral good is the imagination...."

Percy Bysshe Shelley,
A Defence of Poetry

"The whole secret of the study
of nature lies in learning how to use one's eyes."

George Sand,
Nouvelles Lettres d'un Voyageur

"For kindness begets kindness evermore."

Sophocles, *Ajax*

"Kind words can be short and easy to speak, but their echoes are truly endless."

Mother Teresa, *Heart of Joy*

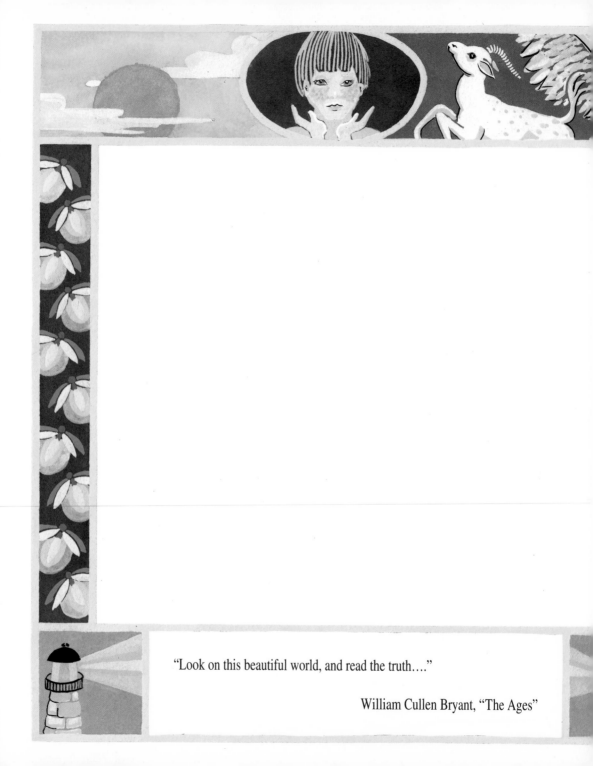

"Look on this beautiful world, and read the truth…."

William Cullen Bryant, "The Ages"

"Truth is not only violated by falsehood; it is outraged by silence."

Henri Frederic Amiel,
Journal Intime

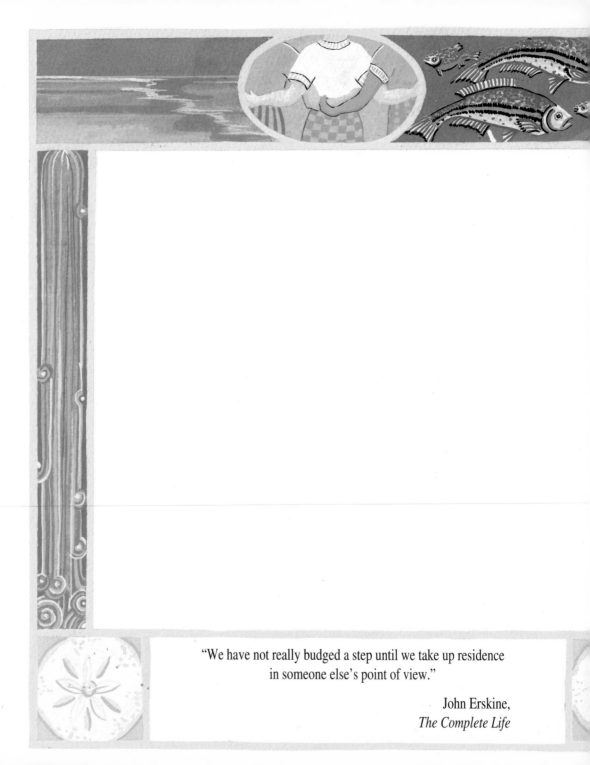

"We have not really budged a step until we take up residence
in someone else's point of view."

John Erskine,
The Complete Life

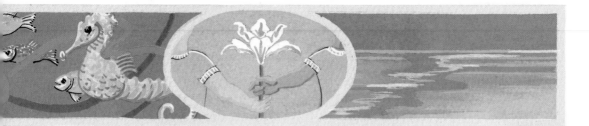

"Peace hath higher tests of manhood
Than battle ever knew."

John Greenleaf Whittier, "The Hero"

"A man should never put on his best trousers
when he goes out to battle for freedom and truth."

Henrik Ibsen, *An Enemy of the People*

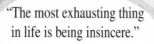

"The most exhausting thing in life is being insincere."

Anne Morrow Lindbergh,
Gift from the Sea

"I am part of all that I have met."

James Joyce, *Ulysses*

"Thou cans't not stir a flower
Without troubling of a star."

Francis Thompson, "The Mistress of Vision"

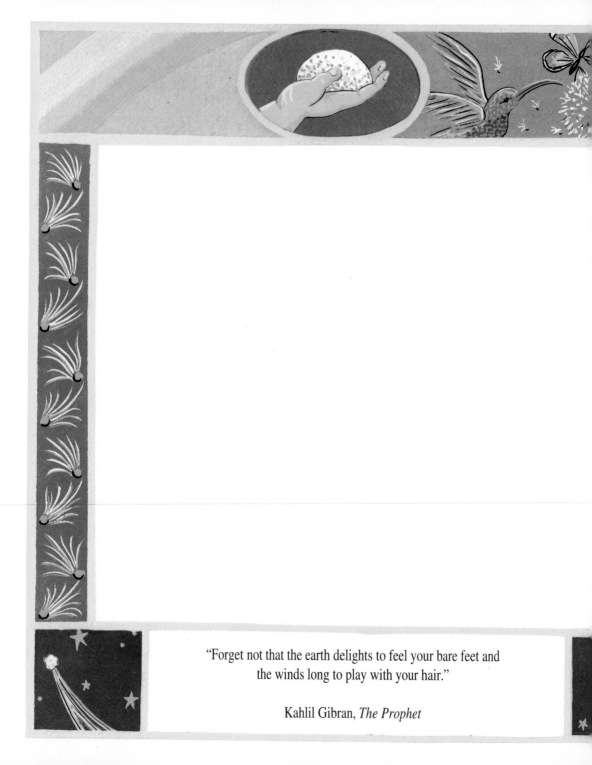

"Forget not that the earth delights to feel your bare feet and
the winds long to play with your hair."

Kahlil Gibran, *The Prophet*

"To see a World in a Grain of Sand
And a Heaven in a Wild Flower:
Hold Infinity in the palm of your hand
And Eternity in an hour."

William Blake,
"Auguries of Innocence"

"Better worlds (I suggest) are born not made;
and their birthdays are the birthdays of individuals."

e. e. cummings, *Six Non-lectures*

"The applause of a single human being is of great consequence."

James Boswell, *Life of Johnson*

"Life is the bow
whose string is the dream."

Romain Rolland,
Journey Within

"My heart leaps up when I behold
A rainbow in the sky;
So was it when my life began;
So it is now I am a man...."

William Wordsworth,
"My Heart Leaps Up"

"No one can be good for long if goodness is not in demand."

Bertolt Brecht, *The Good Woman of Setzuan*

"In spite of everything I still believe that people
are really good at heart."

Anne Frank, *Diary of a Young Girl*

"Rather than love, than money, than fame, give me truth."

Henry David Thoreau,
Walden: Life in the Woods

"Truth will often prevail where there is pains taken to bring it to light."

George Washington,
Maxims

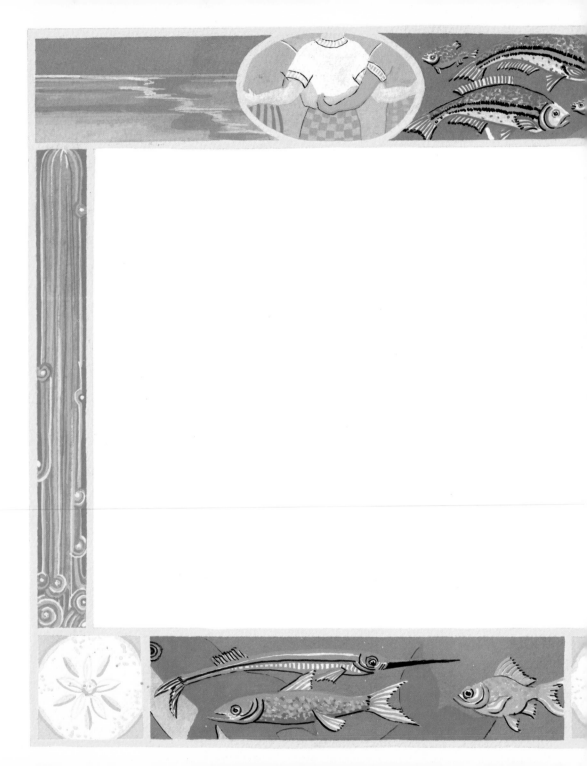

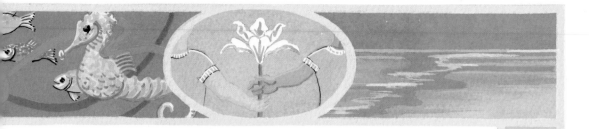

"It isn't much fun being angry /and arguing's just the worst,
so I'm going to say I'm sorry... /just as soon as you say it first."

Jeff Moss, "I'm Going to Say I'm Sorry"

"The love of truth has its reward in heaven and even on earth."

Friedrich Nietzsche, *Beyond Good and Evil*

"What the imagination seizes as Beauty must be truth…."

John Keats,
Letter to Benjamin Bailey, November 22, 1817

"What happens to a man is less significant than what happens within him."

Thomas Mann,
"The Quest of the Bluebird"

"Our true nationality
is mankind."

H. G. Wells,
The Outline of History

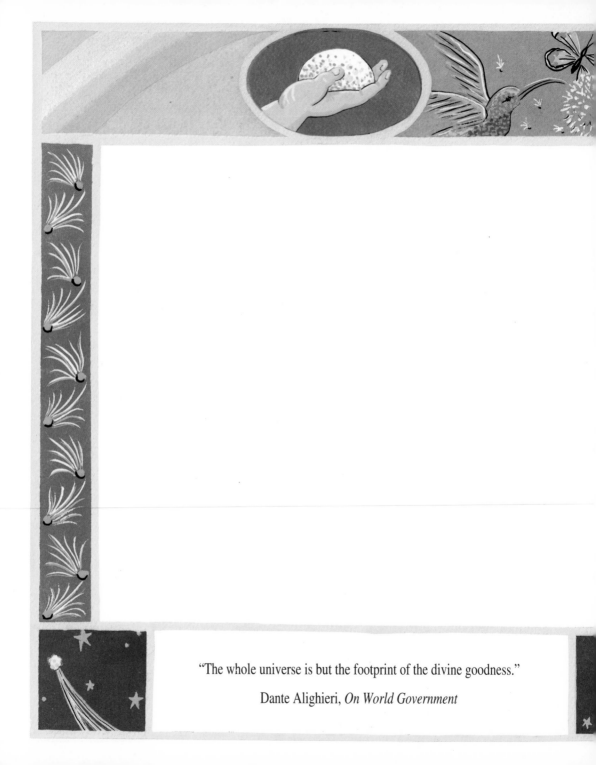

"The whole universe is but the footprint of the divine goodness."

Dante Alighieri, *On World Government*

"A great man is he who does not lose his child's heart."

Mencius, *The Works of Mencius*

*T*o be continued . . .